Narcissism

How To Overcome Fear Of Abandonment, Stop Please
People And Tame Codependent Behavior

(Detection And Disarming Of Gaslight Effect)

Domenic Mcneil

TABLE OF CONTENT

Social Media's Contribution To The Promotion Of Narcissism 1

Living With A Narcissist: A Guide 4

What About The Narcissist? 18

Childhood Adversity And Narcissism 25

Breakup Do's And Don'ts 33

How To Spot A Narcissist 43

Treatment 64

How Quickly Can You Spot A Sociopathic Narcissist Before It's Too Late? 86

Anxiety Disorder Borderline 119

What A Narcissist-Involved Relationship Is Like 138

A Narcissist's Telltale Behavior 148

Social Media's Contribution To The Promotion Of Narcissism

Social media has been under close scrutiny in recent years for its role in the emergence of narcissists. This can't be. Narcissists are not produced by social media, but it does provide a platform for those that are.

Cyber-psychologists that specialize in behavior are in agreement that narcissists may utilize social media because it provides them with the perfect platform to get the respect and adoration they feel they are due.

Researchers have created many sorts of narcissists, which are included in this chapter, not only to acknowledge the existence of a narcissistic personality disorder but also to highlight the main types and sub-types that exist and the contrasts between them.

Grandiose Type and Overt Sub-Type are two sorts of narcissists that are immediately identifiable by most people, while the more subtle Vulnerable Type and Covert Sub-Type are narcissistic types that many people do not believe apply the term "narcissism."

Not every person who has narcissistic characteristics is a typical narcissist. It's not like they suffer from NPD. Even if they are not certifiable and fall short of the diagnostic level requirements, they may nonetheless do significant harm to the features that they do possess.

Narcissists often reject counseling and are generally content with their lives. Since they are not the ones who must cope with the consequences of their problem, they are happier than others who do. Unfortunately, those who are affected by them are the ones who suffer.

A diagnosable narcissist might be someone you're dating, married to, or someone you have in your family, circle of friends, or place of employment.

Hopefully, you now have a better understanding of who they are and what categories they could fit into.

How to comprehend, live with, and maintain your own sanity around a narcissist will be covered in the next chapter.

Living With A Narcissist: A Guide

It cannot be overstated: cohabiting with a narcissist may be a living torment. Living alone is a lot of labor, worry, and misery.

People who live with someone who has narcissistic personality disorder may do so out of love for the person, because the two of them are married and have children, or because of reasons related to their culture or religion. In any case, they must do all in their power to maintain the connection.

To attempt to improve a relationship as much as possible, most individuals ultimately turn to psychological assistance. If you are associated with someone who has NPD, please read that phrase once again. The key term here is "as good as possible." The most that can be expected is that the relationship will be as good as it can be unless you have a narcissist who is open to participating in any kind of treatment to address their narcissistic problem and how it is hurting you, family, friends, and even coworkers.

This is about the fundamental knowledge a person has to have in order to deal with a partner who has narcissistic personality disorder while they are in a relationship with them, if they don't want to leave until they've done everything to make it work.

If you are in a relationship with a narcissist, knowing these three facts will make things much easier:

What it's like to be in a relationship with a narcissist, what's doable, and how to draw boundaries.

What Being with a Narcissist Means

A narcissist's primary concern is raising their level of self-esteem. The self-esteem illness known as narcissism may be conceived of as a condition in which narcissists are persistently uneasy about their relevance, importance, and status.

Although they may seem self-assured on the outside, they are always unsure of their value. Behind the facade of confidence, their self-worth.

In essence, they are more essential to themselves and the enhancement of their self-esteem than anybody or anything else. That includes anybody they have a romantic involvement with.

A narcissist only has two choices when their self-esteem plummets:

They have a depressive episode. Their despair is a self-hating depression, and everything and everyone is affected by the aura that is tied to that energy. They grow haughty, claiming they are flawless, unbeatable, and unique, and they do it at the cost of you and other people. To regain their sense of importance, they undervalue those who are close to them.

The second alternative will, of course, be their preference, and as was already said, you, as the one who is closest to them, will likely be undervalued in order to give them a sense of significance once again.

Because they lack emotional empathy, narcissists don't care whether they do you harm. They don't care and most likely aren't even aware of how you respond when anything is said or done to harm you.

When you complain or say you've been injured by them, they refuse to accept responsibility. They will contest that what they said or did caused you pain. It's probably more your fault. You may have heard the phrase "You're too sensitive" rather often, or they may blame you for forcing them to talk or behave in a specific manner.

This implies that the narcissist will frequently damage your sentiments, whether unintentionally or on design. Being in a relationship with a narcissist is dealing with their lack of empathy, so get used to it. You won't ever hear them apologize.

The capacity to recognize both positive and negative aspects of a person and be able to accept that both exist is known as "whole object relations" (Greenberg, 2017). Narcissists lack this capacity.

Early on, a kid learns to notice both a person's positive and negative traits by imitating their parents, as well as by experiencing their parents' realistic love and acceptance of them despite their flaws.

A person with NPD is capable of achieving this competence if they are motivated and get the right treatment.

NPD sufferers who lack "whole object relations" oscillate between two extreme viewpoints of both themselves and others, and they are either:

Perfect, unique, unbeatable, and entitled (i.e., all-good), or flawed, unworthy, and faulty rubbish (i.e., all-bad)

The narcissist is incapable of seeing you, their partner, in a steady and realistic way. Depending on how people are feeling at the time, they shift back and forth between the two distinct perceptions of you and others: either they are "special" or "worthless" (Greenberg, 2017).

This has nothing to do with you and is not dependent on anything you have done.

The narcissist undoubtedly saw you as faultless, exceptional, and ideal while your relationship was just getting started and in its early phases, living out the illusion of being all-good.

As the relationship progressed and they got to know you more, they saw your flaws (which are universal) and how you were different from their ideal partner.

They would then oscillate between seeing you as severely defective or completely evil.

The absence of "whole object relations" that the narcissist possesses will develop over time; there is only momentary delight. This will have an impact on your relationship's happiness factor and make whatever happiness you two may have had in the past fragile and fleeting.

Because narcissists are unable to maintain a positive, stable picture of you, particularly when they feel wounded, angry, unsatisfied or disappointed by you, the sense of happiness is susceptible to being abruptly shaken (Greenberg, 2017).

They lack "object constancy," which, in essence, means that once they experience anything terrible, whatever good connection you may have with your narcissistic partner is cut off, and all that is positive is thrown out the window.

Your whole past of helping them and being a good person to them has been destroyed and is no longer in their awareness. You are perplexed and wonder how such a full transformation could occur. The sensations of complete love, closeness, and contentment shift in an instant, and your partner starts to dislike you.

Because they lack full object relations, they lack object constancy, which is the reason why this complete about-face occurs.

Recognize that they can only alternate between liking and loathing you because they lack the capacity to observe you, cannot simultaneously notice both your preferred and disliked actions and qualities, and cannot accept of you as a full person.

These contrasting emotions depend on which of your traits or behaviors—those you like or dislike—is active at the time.

This kind of flip could occur when you and your partner are having a romantic evening together without the kids, who are spending the evening with their grandparents. You prepare supper with the intention of watching a movie together later. A "date night" is being held at home.

Dinner was wonderful. The supper was great, and you two spoke for a while about various destinations you plan to take the family in the future.

You make the decision to tidy up the kitchen after supper so you can enjoy the movie without having to worry about it afterwards. Once you're done in the kitchen, you inform your companion that you'll be ready to watch the film in a few minutes.

Unbeknownst to you, your narcissistic partner is starting to act inconsistently in their thoughts because they believe that you are disrupting the evening by cleaning the kitchen while they are getting ready to watch a movie. Your companion becomes irritated because they have to wait for you instead of you dropping everything and going to the theater to see the movie.

As the movie begins, you go outside and take a seat on the sofa to continue your date night with your partner. Your partner is now upset with you for being so rude and making them wait to see the movie. They talk about how your lack of consideration and rudeness makes them believe that you don't love them or value your time together.

You can't believe this is what you got for completing the most basic of tasks—cleaning the kitchen so you could watch the movie without worrying about the cleanup afterwards. To you, it is outrageous to be accused of being careless and unconsiderate when you have always supported your partner.

If you're in a relationship with a narcissist, you're already familiar with how this kind of thing happens and how it makes you feel. If you want to date a narcissist, you should be aware of and ready for the kind of circumstances that were just mentioned. Because you are a different person from your companion, it cannot be avoided and is inevitable.

This indicates that you are unique and possess a vastly varied range of emotions and sensitivities. Your narcissistic partner's insecurities may be sparked by seemingly harmless conduct that you see. Your brief shared sentiments of warmth and fuzzyness are gone. Now when they are enraged, the narcissistic partner starts to diminish you.

You're shocked that your narcissistic partner's whole attitude and manner have abruptly turned 360 degrees while they're busy venting their rage at you. All was okay only a short while ago, but suddenly an argument breaks out as you defend yourself against baseless and egregiously unjust claims.

What About The Narcissist?

When no one else can notice a poisonous relationship, have you ever been in that position? You see a person's poisonous behaviors, but nobody else seems to notice them? Those who fail to see the poison also say things like, "Just let it go." Families apologize. Don't be bothered by it. She is not really saying it.

You offer opportunities as a result of listening to what others around you have to say. You also provide a free pass.

Unfortunately, a poisonous person's actions are not condemned. Everyone around you keeps finding reasons to defend the person. As you watch in perfect quiet, puzzled by what you are seeing. Everyone else continues living their lives in the meanwhile. People dismiss it. They acquiesce in such actions. The poisonous individual, the narcissist, cannot be self-reflective about how their actions are adversely affecting others, hence they will not alter their behavior.

Narcissists see quiet as approval to continue acting in a destructive way since they are not called out for it. This is seen as allowing the narcissist to go on acting in their current manner toward other people. We live in a world of second chances, let's face it. We want to think that people are capable of changing things for the better. We tend to assume the best of individuals much too often.

Giving excellent individuals a second opportunity is perfectly acceptable since they are certainly capable of changing their character and behavior. Giving the narcissists second opportunities, however, is like to giving them a free license to keep up their bad habits. Typically, the phrase "enabling" refers to the field of addictions. By providing booze to an alcoholic or drugs to a drug addict, someone is essentially giving them the go-ahead to continue consuming.

How may this be applied to the world of narcissism? We do, covertly and unknowingly, keep providing the narcissist with narcissistic material. When we give someone our support, we encourage them to go on with behaviors and habits that are often detrimental. By not enforcing sanctions for inappropriate behavior, we might encourage the behavior. Or when we fail to speak out while seeing the harm that these narcissists inflict on others.

By not trusting someone who claims to be a victim of the narcissist, you are also seen as a facilitator of the narcissist. Giving second opportunities and forgiving people are narcissistic need for the narcissist. The more you pardon and give the narcissist second opportunities, the more you let the destructive behavior to persist.

When you attempt to soothe and satisfy the narcissist out of fear of confronting them, you are also aiding the narcissist.

For instance, we constantly give kids the option of where to eat and other activities. Always keep in mind that to satisfy is to allow. Any moment we tolerate someone, we are enabling them, and this is true in all narcissistic relationships. In close relationships, you may help the narcissist by putting up with their behavior or by keeping your emotions to yourself out of consideration for them.

When you keep making excuses for their actions and their unfavorable reactions, it occurs. When a narcissist advances in a company, this occurs because no one wants to kill the golden goose. The aggressive behavior of a narcissist is seen as assertiveness, and their feeling of entitlement is interpreted as assurance. Systems of every sort reward and encourage these behaviors as toxic leaders proliferate in our society.

Sadly, if you expose the narcissist in front of others, you will be gaslighted and used as a scapegoat. As a result, the dynamic is: see something, say nothing. Our culture is encouraging and even praising narcissistic behavior, which is why narcissism is on the rise. Leaders of many organizations and institutions are permitted to get away with it. Insensitive celebrities and influencers are also permitted to get away with it.

Giving the narcissist genuine consequences is the only way to halt narcissistic enabling, but this is difficult to accomplish. Because that is precisely what they want, stop appearing where they are and stop applauding the narcissist. Stop praising their accomplishments and providing them with a platform whenever they seek affirmation. Cut down the air flow! It is that easy to say, yet so difficult to do.

Childhood Adversity And Narcissism

The brain of a youngster may take in anything and start to accept it as fact. Since babies have nothing to compare them to, they accept terrible events as fact, particularly when their caretakers are to blame. A research found that if you spoke to 100 teenagers, at least 80 of them would have experienced some kind of abuse when they were young, which resulted in a mental problem by the time they were adults.

Not every kid has the good fortune to grow up normally, healthily, and carefree. Children can experience all kinds of horrible things, like parent fights, moms being mistreated by alcoholic dads, living in poverty, being ill, and many other things. Additionally, some kids endure sexual abuse—the worst of all negative experiences—quietly for years at a time. Nobody is there for them to confide in about what has been occurring to them. Sadly, a member of the family is the abuser. A youngster who experiences sexual abuse is powerless because they are unaware of what is taking on. They are not to blame for their feelings of guilt and shame. They start to think that they must be flawed for it to be occurring to them. Because they have no idea what to say, they are never able to get up the bravery to tell anybody about it. It's an odd circumstance.

These youngsters have an ingrained idea that they are imperfect and that everyone else is flawless. They feel even worse about themselves when they see other kids their age living in happy, safe families and receiving affection from their grandparents. For them, the fact that they are being treated so obnoxiously is proof that they definitely have a problem. They unknowingly create a highly vengeful demeanor as adults with the unhealed wounds of sexual assault, or any type of trauma for that matter. They never really discover who they are. As a result of the abuse memories being ingrained in their thoughts, people continue to see themselves as being unattractive, beloved, valued, or admirable. They lose all hope of ever experiencing love from anybody if they are repeatedly subjected to abuse, maltreatment, or manipulation by various persons. They believe that everyone is out there with the intention of hurting them or exploiting them in some manner. They thus develop cynicism about life and love.

Now, not everyone with those traits has to develop narcissism. However, narcissistic features, particularly a sensitive kind of narcissism, may emerge in persons who had an unjust and horrible upbringing. Because of their own negative thought patterns and dominating conduct, they are quite prone to feel uneasy and dissatisfied in their relationships. They may end up becoming vindictive, cunning, and unable to control their emotions. They could, for instance, blame their spouses of trivial things all the time and even attempt to discourage them from engaging in their hobbies. They want to seem sad, and they want everyone else to follow suit. They get enraged if they see your happiness and enjoyment of life.

However, it may save a kid from developing any form of personality disorder if abuse of any kind is handled and resolved at a young age and the child feels supported and heard.

Major Traumatic Experiences and Narcissism

Due to some traumatic incidents or experiences in their early lives, some individuals may end up becoming narcissists. While it's not required that everyone who experiences tragedy or injustice at some point develops narcissism, some narcissists have traumatic pasts that continue to influence their conduct into their later years. Narcissists may develop as a result of interpersonal violence, elder siblings who harass younger siblings, long-term abuse of any type, and other factors. Some people struggle to control their emotions, trust others, and show empathy because they have a negative worldview that they have developed through time. They communicate what they experienced during their most vulnerable time in life via their fury and impulsive actions.

So, should you tolerate a narcissist with a difficult past? You could wish to assist them by suggesting that they seek out professional treatment or counseling. However, you shouldn't be responsible for their rude conduct toward you or other people. No matter how much pain a person has experienced, there is never a justification for traumatizing others. They must accept responsibility for their acts and conduct as adults.

Objectivity and Gender

Are males more likely than women to be narcissistic? Okay, sure. There are explanations for it as well. Boys aren't educated to be emotionally intelligent or to have empathy. Always being encouraged to be strong and never weep. They are also expected to excel in their occupations as they mature into men and take on the role of family providers. Because having more money and material possessions would make them feel more strong and self-assured, men are always under pressure to do so. Therefore, if they have a propensity to be so self-absorbed and goal-driven as to even ignore the emotions and sentiments of others, no one questions this.

Women, on the other hand, are seen to be nurturers. They have a responsibility to look after their houses, kids, parents, and in-laws. There are fewer women who are narcissists than males because they are socialized to think that selflessness and sacrifice are the norm. Today's world is progressively changing, however. Now, narcissism is often seen in women as well. There are certain women who don't mind being conniving, selfish, cruel, domineering, and very shallow.

Therefore, both men and women may be prevented from becoming narcissists if they are taught to be conscious of their feelings and to not be afraid to express them appropriately. In order to prevent children from being influenced by what society teaches them, parents and other adults should keep an eye out for them and work to instill the proper values in them from an early age.

Breakup Do's And Don'ts

You can feel conflicted about saying goodbye to someone in the event that you're thinking about doing so. You did get together on purpose, after all.

Therefore, considering "Will things improve?" is often assumed. Would it be wise for me to give it another chance? "Will I regret this decision?" Making the decision to break up is not simple. You could need to get some room to think about it.

Separating involves having an unusual or difficult conversation, whether or whether you are confident in your decision. The person to whom you are bidding goodbye could feel wounded, discouraged, depressed, discarded, or heartbroken.

When you're the one ending the relationship, you probably think you should do it in a thoughtful and sensitive way. You don't believe the other person should suffer harm, and you would prefer not to be bothered by the same thing.

Do You Need to Avoid It? Or, rather, just end it?

Some people avoid the unpleasant task of starting a contentious conversation. Some people have a "fair get it over with" attitude. However, none of these approaches is the most effective.

Avoiding just serves to prolong the situation (and may end up worsening the other person's situation). Furthermore, if you rush into a contentious conversation without giving it enough thought, you can say things you later regret.

The greatest thing is something in the middle:

Think things out so you are aware of the reasons you need to end your relationship. then take action at that moment.

Dos and Don'ts of Divorce

Every situation is different. There is no one method that works for everyone to handle separation. In any event, if you start to consider having the breakup conversation, there are some general "do's and don'ts" you might keep in mind.

DO:

1. Give your needs and reasons for needing them careful thought. Make time to reflect on your feelings and the motivations behind your decision.

2. Always be honest with yourself. It's OK to make the best option for you, even though the other person may be hurt by it.

3. You only need to handle it delicately. Think about what you'll say and the

possible reactions from the other person. Will it surprise your BF or GF? Miserable? Distraught? Hurt? Or maybe you even feel better?

Being sensitive may be facilitated by taking into account the other person's viewpoint and feelings. You may also use it to help you prepare. Do you think the person you're bidding goodbye to could cry? a change in attitude? How would you handle that kind of reaction?

4. You mean well. Let them know how much you value the person in question.

5. Consider the traits you should exhibit for the other person, such as reliability, generosity, responsiveness, respect, and

awareness. Tell the truth, but don't be brutal.

6. Express your admiration for the other person and the qualities that first drew you to them.

7. After that, explain why you should continue. "Genuineness" does not mean "cruel." To understand why something isn't working, avoid dissecting the traits of the other person. Think of sensitive and gentle ways to express the truth while yet being nice.

8. Let's take it on the chin. You've shared a lot of knowledge with one another. Consider that and break up face-to-face to demonstrate your excellent qualities. If you live far away, consider a video

visit or, if all else fails, just pick up the phone.

It may seem easy to separate via Facebook or chat. In any event, consider how you'd feel and what your friends would think of that person's characteristics if they did it to you as your boyfriend or girlfriend!

9. If it helps, confide in someone you know to be reliable. It might help when you discuss your feelings with a trusted friend. However, make sure the person you trust can keep it a secret until you and your BF or GF have your real separation conversation.

10. Ensure that you are the one to say it to your BF/GF, not someone else. That is

one reason parents, older sisters or brothers, and other adults may be the best conversation partners. They won't talk incoherently or ignore it.

DON'T:

1. Make an effort not to avoid the other person or the conversation you truly want to have.

2. Prolonging a situation is difficult in the long run for both you and your BF or GF. Additionally, when people procrastinate, information may leak in any case. You never need to wait for the person with whom you are breaking up to hear it from someone else before telling them yourself.

3. Avoid jumping into a contentious conversation without giving it careful thought. You could say things you regret.

4. Aim to avoid offending. Talk respectfully about your former (or potential ex). Be careful not to gossip about or disparage that individual. Consider your feelings. You'd think that now that you're not together, your ex would only say certain things about you.

Furthermore, no one can tell for certain since your ex may become a friend or you might attempt to rekindle an emotion in the future.

These "rules and regulations" don't only apply to divorce. If someone invites you out but you're not really interested, you may follow the same guidelines for politely declining their invitation.

How To Spot A Narcissist

Contrary to common assumption, since narcissism has so many facets, it is not always simple to comprehend. Actually, not all narcissists behave as if they rule the world. Some of them are so cunning that they can hide their arrogance and show phony interest in others in order to draw attention to themselves.

Sometimes narcissism is shown via rage, exhilaration, or a combination of the two. Narcissists have a number of characteristics in common, including an excess of self-assurance, self-absorption, self-praise, and grandiloquence.

Current cultural trends have made it easier to readily self-promote online through social media networks, for example, which has aided in the growth of narcissism. Finding someone who is not a narcissist may be harder today than finding one who is, given the issue that is now prevalent.

Talking to a Narcissist

Simply striking up a discussion with someone might reveal whether or not they are a narcissist. You'll notice that the discussion will constantly return to him talking about himself if you start out on a subject other than him. The narcissist is also unable to listen to others discuss subjects unrelated to him.

Any narcissist's favorite subject is naturally themselves. A narcissist will try to take the upper hand in a discussion about anything else by repeatedly cutting off the other person or waiting until they have finished speaking before launching onto a totally unrelated subject (which will almost certainly be about themselves again).

They have trouble empathizing with other individuals and often dismiss the perspectives and experiences of others. When you are speaking with a narcissist, you will also note that they often name-drop in an effort to come out as superior. This might include having the appropriate connections, attending famous institutions, and belonging to elite clubs. The narcissist has no trouble boasting.

The Relationships of a Narcissist

You should also consider the connections that a narcissist keeps up. They often struggle to maintain mutually beneficial long-term connections and typically only have superficial friendships. They often stay with those who are always praising and admiring of them.

How severe narcissism is

You will notice that there are "mild" and "severe" narcissists when it comes to their demeanor. On the surface, some of them might seem to be extremely personable and charming, but there are others of them who are snobs who like disparaging others and talking about them behind their backs. The worst aspect is that narcissists lack self-reflection since they are oblivious of their disorder. They believe that their actions are appropriate and natural, and they find it difficult to understand why other people do not find them appealing, nice, etc.

You will be rather charmed by how a social narcissist conducts themselves, and you may want to go out with them more often if you chance to be well acquainted with one. But be caution since narcissists often use manipulation to further their own ends. When a narcissist determines that you are useless to them, they will often just discard you and refuse to interact with you.

The narcissist loves to reside in urban areas where individualistic culture is prevalent. They have a great preference for self-aggrandizing entertainment, like reality TV programs, and their concept of leadership would be to exploit and control their subordinates rather than contributing to the hard labor.

You're in for a nasty fight if you try to disrespect a narcissist. Even constructive criticism is never welcomed by them. Some of them pretended to take it gracefully, but they would later vent their resentment over it and try to defend their own actions. When you tell a narcissist that they are not as smart or as handsome as they believe they are, they will get quite angry since they prefer to be adored than to be loved by others.

Take note of a person's body language who you believe to be a narcissist. Typically, they hold themselves haughtily and display an inflated ego at all times, particularly when they perceive a danger to their self-esteem. They also often use big hand movements when speaking.

Find out whether a person exhibits unconditional love to anybody else in order to evaluate whether or not they are a narcissist. Only those whom one has nothing to gain, such as a vulnerable animal or an elderly family, are shown unconditional affection. Anyone or everything that won't assist a narcissist fulfill their selfish ambitions will not be given their time or attention.

Among other symptoms, the complex mental health issue known as narcissistic personality disorder (NPD) is characterized by an exorbitant need for praise and attention.

Narcissistic tendencies, often known as NPD, are defined by a pattern of domineering behavior that includes emotional and verbal abuse.

Narcissistic manipulation examples include:

Triangulation. Someone who wishes to include a third party in your argument to promote their own point of view will use this tactic.

Gaslighting. A person attempting to gaslight you may often falsify information or claim that events you recall didn't truly happen in an effort to make you doubt your own perspective and reality.

Hoovering. Through this tactic, an unhealthy or abusive relationship is attempted to be rekindled or lured back into.

Silent treatment. It becomes manipulation when someone purposefully ignores you in an effort to gain control over you or to make you feel alone.

Scapegoating. Parents who are narcissistic, manipulative, and motivated by self-esteem may pick out one child as the offender.

Passive animosity Subliminal narcissistic manipulation may be identified by the use of sarcastic language, sabotage, and indirect blame-shifting.

These tactics have the capacity to confuse you, make you question reality, and undermine your sense of self.

The term "narcissistic victim syndrome" refers to the distinct and usually severe effects of narcissistic manipulation. Even though narcissistic abuse is not a recognized mental health condition, many experts concur that it may have a significant, long-lasting impact on mental health.

Do not forget that narcissism and abuse are not often linked. Numerous abusers do not have NPD, and abusive behavior is not always indicative of having NPD.

No matter what, a mental health issue can never excuse abusive conduct. People choose to abuse and dominate others, and narcissistic characteristics or any other personality condition don't always translate into violent behavior.

Narcissistic abuse indicators

They first seem to be flawless.

Regardless of the kind of relationship, narcissistic abuse often follows a pattern that is predictable, but it may occur in a variety of ways.

2019 study shows that after you've fallen deeply and quickly in love, this violence often begins.

It makes sense why you did. While love bombing, they gave the impression of being kind, courteous, and giving. To make you feel special and adored, they lavished you with adoring remarks, passionate gestures, and expensive gifts.

It's conceivable that at this first stage you felt so intense and overwhelming that you didn't pause to consider if they would be too fantastic. Then, over time, negging or other dishonest techniques began to take the place of gifts and declarations of affection.

Narcissistic parents may also provide you love, adoration, praise, and money if you don't do anything to annoy them and lose their favor. They then use tactics like gas lighting, quiet treatment, and negging much too often.

People don't think the abuse really occurred.

Abuse and manipulation committed by narcissists are usually subtle. It's possible that these behaviors are so well concealed while occurring in public that nobody who hears or sees them recognizes them as abusive.

You could still not completely understand what is happening even then. You just recognize how perplexed, annoyed, or even guilty you feel about your "mistakes."

A narcissistic parent may softly ask, "Are you sure you want dessert?" As an alternative, they may call you clumsy and make fun of you. You just lack the ability to stop yourself, right? To make the insult seem genuine, they touch your shoulder and join the group laughter.

You would assume that your loved ones would accept you. Unfortunately, however, this isn't always the case. Even while they may not dispute with your assessment that you were mistreated, your loved ones can be curious in how you interpret what occurred or comfort you that you must have misunderstood what happened. They wouldn't ever intend to hurt you.

This ambiguity might be very harmful. It might make you doubt if the abuse truly took place and lead you to lose faith in your loved ones. It's possible that you misunderstood what they said or misinterpreted their facial expression.

They've started a smear campaign.

People with narcissistic traits usually feel the need to maintain their appearance of perfection in order to continue receiving compliments from others. They could try to damage your reputation to achieve this.

They may reply when you start bringing up problems or criticizing their behavior by:

openly expressing their anger at you by calling you names, threatening you, and motivating others to be critical of you

The narcissist makes up stories about your "destructive" or "unstable" conduct to convey to your loved ones in an effort to discredit you. What's worse is that if you respond angrily (and who wouldn't?) they may use it to bolster their falsehoods.

Narcissists typically possess a gift for charm. That persona they first presented to you? Everyone else keeps seeing that.

They often get your loved ones' support by forcefully asserting that they only have your best interests at heart. If you attempt to justify the abuse to your loved ones, they could disagree with you.

You feel alone.

If your loved ones don't understand, you'll probably feel rather alone, which makes you more open to more narcissistic manipulation. The abuser may attempt to win you back by being kind, offering an apology if necessary, or by behaving as if nothing had occurred.

"Hoovering," as it is sometimes referred as, typically works best when you are alone. You are more prone to start doubting your views of the abuse if you are unable to talk about the abuse with anybody.

If your loved ones reach out to you, tell you that you erred, and encourage you to give the abusive relationship another opportunity, you could opt to do so just to restore your connection with family and friends.

You stop moving.

Different individuals respond differently to trauma and different types of abuse.

You may try to defend yourself against the aggressor or you could flee (flight). If these tactics don't work or you don't feel like you have the skills to use them, you can respond by fawning or frozen.

The freeze reflex commonly happens if you feel powerless. It typically involves dissociation because it may help minimize the intensity of the abuse, numbing some of the pain and suffering you feel.

Although freezing might be favorable in certain situations, it isn't actually helpful if you have a method to escape danger. Though you could decide to remain if you believe there is no other option, you might even respond by gushing over or making attempts to placate your partner.

You have trouble making decisions.

If you are often criticized and devalued, you may have extremely poor self-esteem and confidence.

The implication of narcissistic manipulation is typically that you continuously make bad decisions and are unable to do any task successfully. In an untruly affectionate tone, an abusive spouse may call you names directly, such as "Honey, you're so foolish. How would you manage without my help?

Over time, you can start to absorb these slights and link them to the way you see yourself, which will make you constantly question yourself.

If someone employs gas lighting tactics, you can start to doubt your judgment. (It is explained here how to respond.)

If someone manages to deceive you into believing you dreamed events that truly occurred, you might continue to doubt your understanding of what happened. This ambiguity may make it harder for you to make decisions in the future.

Treatment

A psychotherapist or therapist who specializes in treating this particular form of personality disorder is often involved in the long-term process of treating this disease. People with crippling symptoms, such as depression or anxiety disorders, which are often linked to the disease, might be administered medications. In serious situations, hospitalization can be required. Let's start with this scenario first and get it out of the way since it is the most terrifying. Just know that you most likely won't need this intensive therapy.

Hospitalization

If this disease is serious, the person may need to stay in the hospital for a while before their threatening symptoms may be treated with medicine or treatment. A temporary solution for people who could be impulsive or even self-destructive is hospitalization. Poor reality testers could also need hospitalization in order to rule out the presence of many disorders. Hospitalizations are often short and focused on the particular symptom at hand rather than the complete disease.

Additionally, patients who lack the motivation to finish their treatment plan or who have a precarious social or object connection could need hospitalization. People who engage in damaging, persistent activities could also need therapy that requires a hospital stay.

Small patient and staff groups will meet regularly in institutions and host community forums where patients may express their feelings to the group. We will always consider what they have to say. To assist patients with their issues, there will be both productive job assignments and leisure activities. The patients will be able to direct their distressing feelings and impulses here into the hospital so that by the time they leave, they will feel elevated and weightless.

The purpose of hospitalization is to strengthen the patient's will so they may become more self-aware, feel more connected to others, and be able to identify their narcissistic tendencies in order to overcome them.

Psychosocial Support

The fundamental goal of psychosocial therapy, often known as talk therapy, is to help the patient become aware of their narcissistic tendencies. If both hospitalization and psychological therapy are required, they will be carried out concurrently; if not, the patient may get psychosocial care elsewhere.

Psychosocial treatment, sometimes known as psychotherapy, comes in two varieties. Both solo and group lessons are available.

Individual

The practitioner and the patient will speak candidly about the patient's symptoms, anxieties, and what they can do to feel better about themselves throughout individual sessions. Psychotherapy often involves two individuals having a basic talk rather than something more unusual like hypnosis.

The patient's narcissistic tendencies could even be avoided by the therapist in favor of talking about issues that are more general or entirely unrelated to the patient's life. If you are a patient in a psychotherapy session, follow the advice of the therapist and pay attention to their recommendations.

Group

The group-based approach to treating narcissistic personality disorder involves bringing together people who have a same problem or who may have various personality disorders. Because group therapy seems to be the more successful treatment option, it is more widely used. It seems that those who have the personality disorder will also become more aware of it after seeing others behaving in narcissistic ways. They are better able to identify their signs and actions, and they will learn empathy much more quickly.

In order to provide certain group members the freedom to separate from the group if they feel they must, group therapy may include more than one therapist.

Lifestyle and DIY treatments

Minor narcissists might genuinely modify their lifestyles and use home cures for their problems. You may attempt some of these treatments at home if the problem is not severe. Keep an open mind, adhere to a treatment plan if one has been offered to you, study about the disease, and get therapy for any mental health issues or drug misuse that may be aggravating the personality disorder, however.

Here are a few things you may do to cure your narcissistic personality disorder on your own at home.

Stress Reduction

Although most of us think of narcissistic people as being too optimistic and self-assured, the truth is that they are often very stressed out people. This may seem unproductive. Therefore, picking up some stress-reduction skills might be beneficial.

If you believe that stress may be the root of your narcissism, consider some of the treatments listed below.

Meditation

There are many other types of meditation, but I'm just going to discuss the easiest one here so you can start.

Locate a calm, distraction-free area in your house or outdoors where you can concentrate. It is essential to switch off any mobile phones, iPads, TVs, or other technological gadgets that might distract you from your meditation practice.

Now take a seat comfortably on the floor or in a chair, but don't lay down! In case you lay down, you could nod off. You have a choice of sitting with your legs out or fully extended in the lotus position. It doesn't matter as long as you're at ease.

Focus on your breathing while closing your eyes. Don't attempt to alter the pace of your breathing at this time. Simply be mindful of it there.

Try to then regulate your breathing. Take a deep breath in for seven seconds, hold it for three, and then exhale slowly for five seconds. Repeat numerous times until you notice a decrease in your heart rate and your attention is only on your breathing.

Simply dismiss any thoughts that arise without passing judgment. Don't judge yourself or get angry just because you had an idea. They will sometimes interrupt the session and are normal.

When you feel at ease once again, spend a few seconds to spread your legs before standing.

Yoga

If you are new to yoga, you may want to look for some courses to join so that you can learn the correct stretches. Find an internet video that demonstrates the motions if doing them in front of people makes you uncomfortable.

T'ai Chi

You've seen tai chi if you've watched folks in the park moving slowly and smoothly into various stances. To learn, you can look up a few postures and motions online or enroll in a class.

Maintain Your Concentration

It is possible to recover from this illness, but it will need patience and effort. Making manageable objectives, such as finding an online yoga video, will help you remain motivated. Once you've achieved that, another objective would be to finish the first yoga video class for beginners that you come across. Remind yourself often of your objectives and the fact that you may mend your connections with people and become a happy person.

Stay Upbeat

Narcissists are often mistaken for having great levels of confidence and self-esteem, but in reality, they don't. So, throughout your therapy and the rest of your life, strive to have a cheerful attitude. Always look for the positive in things and use some kind of physical or mental technique to force yourself to stop thinking negatively.

The wrist-rubber band technique is something you may attempt. Snap the rubber band to remind yourself that you should be thinking positively whenever you catch yourself in a cycle of negative thoughts.

You ought to be able to overcome this personality condition and have a better, more meaningful life with the help of home remedies and outpatient therapy. Let's look at how to handle a narcissist if you are not one yourself but interact with them professionally or personally.

Knowing How to Spot Narcissistic Behavior

Because narcissism and confidence are so closely intertwined, it may be hard to recognize when the behavior goes too far. Ensure that you are attentively observing these behaviors. Additionally, be careful to be mindful of any triggers that may emerge while interacting with this individual. A narcissist is prone to experience triggers or discomfort in circumstances that a normal person would not. When making judgments, these situations are evident. A narcissist will be unable to take any kind of constructive criticism, despite the fact that there are many different methods to do it.

Even if it is intended to be helpful, passing judgment on someone with NPD generally results in a negative reaction. The person may exhibit intense defensiveness and may even revert to using derogatory language. These hasty responses are excellent illustrations of how a narcissist thinks. Any criticism is seen as a statement to the effect that "you aren't good enough."

Although it is a more severe example, remember that narcissism may manifest itself in other ways as well. Have you ever conversed with someone just on their terms? It is a narcissistic trait to just be interested in talking about oneself and not care about what the other person has to say. Although this is more unpleasant than anything else, be aware that over time it may hurt your feelings. It will be more difficult to disrupt a narcissist's tendencies the longer they may continue.

In certain cases, you could even see that a narcissist is living in a distorted version of reality. Living with the conviction that everything revolves around you is frequent in NPD. This undoubtedly appears silly to other people. However, there is no other way to live for a narcissist. Everyone affected by this style of thinking, including the NPD sufferer, is in danger. It's crucial to keep a narcissist anchored in reality, particularly when perception is already so distorted.

Another method a narcissist will satisfy their need for fulfillment is by fishing for praises. A useful sort of praise that ought to come easily is being complemented. A narcissist may act in a certain way only to elicit positive feedback from another individual. Naturally, the unjust pressure that is linked diminishes the authenticity of the activity.

Helping a Narcissist

The most efficient method to deal with any form of mental illness is always to seek expert care. A professional is the one with the best grasp of what can be going on in a narcissist's thinking since the condition is more complicated than most people realize. A doctor may provide NPD sufferers treatment alternatives and drug regimens, among other things. These techniques are, of course, situational. Affordable healthcare is not available to everyone, and narcissists are never aware such a problem even exists. But you may be wondering what you can do to assist.

One strategy to establish healthy boundaries is to refuse to comply with unjust demands. Setting these limits is crucial when dealing with narcissism. An someone with NPD may not even be aware that they are expecting too much from others. Be careful to defend yourself if you often find yourself among narcissists. You will need to equalize the connection and make sure that it is occurring in the most reciprocal manner possible, so know that it is alright to say "no." No matter how pleasant or persuasive the other person may seem, make sure you maintain your position.

Be as delicate as you can while dealing with any circumstance. Remember that someone with NPD will probably be rather delicate on the inside while having a robust façade. If you believe that you are being treated unjustly, bring this up in casual conversation rather than trying to fight fire with fire. Explain how the conduct is affecting you and why it is giving you this feeling. The best method to explain oneself without assigning blame is to start with your own sentiments. Allow the narcissist to consider the fact that they are the ones making you feel this way.

Recognize that changes are inevitable. You and your relationships with the narcissist may be having a great time, but everything may change in a heartbeat. If you want to retain these connections, which are often unexpected, you must be prepared to evolve along with them. NPD patients are likely to be used to taking the lead. Be prepared for significant behavioral changes if you express your power in return. Keep in mind that your goal is not to make the other person feel awful. Simply by refusing to give in to pressure, you are maintaining your integrity.

Make an effort not to personalize anything. This might be challenging, particularly if a love connection is involved, but remember that your happiness should not completely depend on the satisfaction of another person. A narcissist will probably annoy you as much as they will attract you. It is a special dualism that might be difficult for outsiders to comprehend. Because of this, it's critical to maintain a strong sense of self. Recognize your value and understand that extreme narcissistic behavior is harmful.

When someone has narcissism, it shows in their overconfidence and sense of entitlement. They believe they are perfect and can do no wrong. This is over the top conduct that breathes and radiates conceit, pretentiousness, and a deeply ingrained sense of unjustified superiority. "I am unique. Because they are not me, everyone else in the world is beneath me. People with narcissistic traits are often characterized as arrogant, conceited, self-absorbed, and impolite. They see the world as a stage for playing with emotions, as an untapped resource to take advantage of, and as a field where the truth can be bent to their will. They may be considered "winners," yet because of their self-described perfection, they are disagreeable people to be around. Thus, they are also liars. The majority of the time, their success is a result of their utter contempt for other people and their sentiments. Or, to put it another way, narcissists will ignore how others are feeling and push through them. Other individuals are impediments in their eyes. We are essentially the next obstacle they must overcome. If it meant that they would get just a little bit farther ahead of everyone else, they would probably shove us over the edge of a top-floor balcony.

Narcissists are notorious for often breaking up conversations. They continuously want to be in the spotlight and believe that they are deserving of it at all times. They want attention. They want to be understood. They strive to take the lead in all local gatherings, professional and social networks, and enormous masses. They are the individuals that exude confidence at all times. They are really endearing individuals who are often fairly humorous and snarky. They make pleasant company in public, but when they go home and into their own comfort zones, they trade in their endearing exteriors for the pompous, emotionally depleted ones they wear when they return to their personal spaces. With their extensive use of manipulation and outlandish but convincing falsehoods as a technique, narcissists may nearly be described as fanatics.

Narcissists have such a strong sense of self-worth. But below it all is a person who has been profoundly impacted by life. Narcissists are people, albeit pretty hard-core ones, who have been molded by past trauma, past experiences, or past abuse. This, in turn, has crafted them into a person with such anxiety that the line between nervousness and abandonment has morphed and blurred into a singularly, individualistic focus that the adulation that they are constantly seeking is due to their inner mental conflicts that were borne from a solitary and possibly unloved childhood. They have evolved what we may term externally spotlighted hubris as a result of this. Simply said, this is what a spotlight is. Some kind of internal spotlight that turns on or externalizes when it feels the need to be seen. It burns so brightly that it compels others to change their attention and give the narcissist their whole attention. If seen from a psychological angle, children under the age of 10 are most likely to exhibit this personality or behavioral attribute. The phase our brains go through throughout early childhood development may best be associated to the behavior-type of boastfulness or to brag about something. It is the urge to stand out from the crowd, to seek attention, whether that is from your parents, your family, or your friends. A narcissist basically brags about themselves when they do so.

A narcissist is someone we all know. They may be our mother or father; they might have behaved in this manner for as long as we can remember, leaving us, as adults, broken, baffled, and worn out. They might have been our brother or sister; they were constantly praised and told they were the star; they were serial winners and cultivated an egotism that has become the potential source of problems in our lives and is still having an impact on us now. They could be a coworker or employee. But where does narcissism come from? Why does it produce individuals who are so self-absorbed, and where does it originate from? Go back now.

How Quickly Can You Spot A Sociopathic Narcissist Before It's Too Late?

Narcissistic Partner Warning Signs
There are several techniques one may use to determine if the person they share a home with is a narcissist. However, not all individuals who exhibit narcissistic features are narcissistic by nature. Everyone has a strong tendency to adore oneself. Nobody on earth does not value or love themselves.

In reality, even individuals who lack narcissistic traits have the power to do more devastation on society than do narcissists themselves. On the other hand, family members shouldn't be trusted to diagnose this disease. This is due to the worry that there would be prejudice in the family and that the diagnosis may breed animosity or long-lasting resentment, which would ultimately bring division.

A Narcissist Will Be Against examination or diagnosis

Exposing someone to check up is one method you may use to determine whether someone is a narcissist. This is a result of their tendency to be more jubilant than those in their family structure. Because they are not held responsible for their acts, they do not see any shortcomings in their life. On the other side, individuals around them take on the burden of their diseases so they do not directly experience their effects.

Due to the agony, one can only look for a diagnosis. These individuals are unable to look for such since they will not identify themselves in any manner with such; as a consequence, it might be challenging to diagnose these people in certain cases. Therefore, conclusions have often been drawn based on statements made by persons in their immediate vicinity as well as the fact that their traits fit into the category of narcissist behaviors or situations.

Even when there is nothing in reality, they need approval in areas where they feel they have excelled.

This quality is essential. Occasionally, individuals tend to overemphasize things until it seems that they are starting to become worried. People may initially put up with such conduct, but with time they will have seen the pattern. This pattern will result in a diagnosis. Members who wish to investigate the cause of this oddity will criticize those who don't.

Since this is a common trait among most individuals, it is the trend rather than the individual that is helpful. In most cases, when someone is too demanding of praise yet is not deserving of it, it paints an image of some flaw in that person. The best method for determining if a person has narcissism is to use this formula.

They dominate conversations and disparage inferiors.

For the majority of narcissists of any kind, this is an extremely potent feature. It is in their nature to put themselves above everyone else for their own personal gain. A narcissist will never participate in a discussion by sitting down to listen. Instead, despite the fact that he may not be familiar with the subject, he will want to be the primary contributor.

His motivation is to induce a detour from the primary list by incorporating his characteristics and traits into the discussion, therefore he doesn't really care about the talk's main purpose.

Instead of allowing you to talk about issues that impact the community or anything else, he would rather that you listen to him brag about his accomplishments. In any event, he will demonstrate to you how you cannot do anything without his participation since he believes he is the only one who has answers to all current problems. In order for him to continue being featured on that subject, he will demonstrate to you how pointless, irrelevant, and invalid your contributions to the matter are.

Anyone who feels devalued may leave the meeting or maybe break down in tears over it. He disparages them and boasts that he can manage issues without them in order to earn social capital by picking on the weaker members of society. His conceit and haughtiness give him joy.

They Lack Remorse and Are Very Courageous

They have no need to apologize to the friends and relatives they offended unless doing so would benefit them. They don't have time to spend if they are aware that acting regretfully will not benefit them in any way. Whatever they do or say has no repercussions for them and is final. Even if they experience the repercussions, they will always find a way to shift the blame and ask others to bear their burden.

They don't have the word "sorry" in their language. Instead, they think that because it is their responsibility to serve others, they must always accept apology for the wrongs done to them by others.

They Exude Great Arrogance

This is in keeping with how things usually work. They believe they are in great authority over everyone on earth and that the planet was created only for them. As long as you are in their vicinity, it makes no difference who you are or what you do to them. They'll try to make you seem tiny and underqualified. He could remark something to the effect that dating you is a favor they are doing for you since they believe you are not theirs.

In some cases, they become violent and uncontrolled. As long as they are feared and given that importance in everything, they will proudly respond to problems even if they are aware of the proper course of action.

Narcissists experience insecurity.

A narcissist doesn't like being despised, and he also thinks there are many reasons why someone may dislike him. When they are not first and foremost adored, they become quite insecure. Every time anything occurs that would give them the sense that you are superior to them, they will respond by being extremely hostile toward you.

They have every right to be envious of you, but when someone else is, they become very uneasy.

They live in an imaginary world and have an imaginative life.

They believe that no one could possibly be so superior to them in this world. They believe that if given the chance, they can fix any problem. A narcissist would use fantasies to the point of cheating to describe his accomplishments in as much detail as possible as long as he gets his mileage.

As far as the connection is concerned, it is the best he can provide. There is no use in arguing with this personality since the likelihood is that he will win and leave you feeling humiliated, inferior, and ashamed, or you will wind up giving him needless credit.

Techniques for Dealing with Narcissistic Individuals

Knowing that the individual you are dealing with is a narcissist may substantially assist you in avoiding many unavoidable situations. It's like removing your own yoke before it encircles your neck. Because this person needs to feel loved and valued no matter what the situation, it is also important to be aware of the steps you may take to interact with them in a more loving manner. It is challenging to modify them since it goes against their nature and, by extension, the nature of their disease.

Being loved and valued as an integral part of you is their only drug:
a) Recognize and respect the complexity of their connection.
You must first comprehend the nature of their functioning. Treat people differently by abstaining from breaching their boundaries, particularly in areas where they feel vulnerable. You must keep your distance from them as much as possible. It may not be that simple, however, since these individuals have a tendency to become very close to you

and will want to feel quite alone if you maintain your distance from them.

As long as you are protected, it doesn't matter how they feel or what they may say. You may securely remain with them if you do this.

b) You must realize that they dislike being questioned, whether outright or covertly. Any time a narcissist feels challenged, resentment will surface.

They could ultimately persuade others to band together against you. You shouldn't become discouraged and frightened by such behavior; what you need to understand is that he is only attempting to allay his concerns by staging a drama. However, you must identify your boundaries and convey them to others in a fearless manner.

Despite the fact that they could feel more uneasy, you should still let them know your limits. Finding a discreet location is necessary if you feel the need to alter such characteristics. When you rebuke or advise them in front of others, they may get upset, make a fuss, and perhaps reject your advice altogether.

b) attempting to change the way they operate is like to attempting to pull a pig out of the mud. Hey, it could seem like it heard you, but in the end, you'll just have wasted your time since you'll be forced to adapt.

d) You should surround yourself with persons who are aware of the circumstances and are prepared to support your plan of action. These folks will assist you in putting out any fire that the narcissist's mood swings may cause to flare up.

The Numerous Aspects of a Narcissist

Narcissists have two distinct personalities. their outward behavior, outward look, and interior, or secret, aspects of their lives. On the outside, they exhibit this feeling of entitlement and power, so they demand a lot of special treatment based on the presumption that they are so successful and ought to be respected. However, they have a deep feeling of insecurity and are sensitive to criticism, which results in some unsettling emptiness and shamefulness.

Due to their fear of failure and criticism, they seek for covert means of defending themselves from external assaults. They need to find a means to shield themselves from the risks associated with the effects of their actions and words since they are aware that they are leading a life full of falsehoods.

The important thing to remember is that narcissists have little to no empathy for other people, if any at all.

How the Narcissistic Partner Abuses You

It often occurs that individuals become victims of events, particularly narcissistic abuse. Your life reaches a point when you begin to feel squandered and twisted. At this point, you are being ruthlessly violated, defrauded, and maybe ridiculed, which gives you the impression that you are living in a dream.

You have a lot of faith in someone, yet you feel that your investment in his life has been a complete waste. It has been broken down into countless worthless pieces. You feel as if your "self" has been beaten up and that you have been minimized. Maybe you were replaced at some point, and your work was abandoned.

Even if you may not physically see the markers to support your narrative, it is preferable to have a good breakup than to endure this terrible period of time caused by the deliberate destruction of your morals and sense of who you are as a person. All you experience is a sensation of twisted recollections, a sense of being torn apart, and maybe the presence of scars.

Targets' Qualities
Weakness and Delicacy in Emotions
The Emotional Fragility: The Endless Secrets to Recognizing and Developing Your Id

Emotional delicacy and emotional affectability are very different. You may, to a greater or lesser extent, possess affectability. The dearth of resources for coping with your most complex inner states is made much worse by delicacy. As a result, being delicate entails having a lot of trouble coping with even the smallest daily challenges.

For a meaningful explanation, we only described how those two concepts vary. Many people make an effort to standardize their emotional sensitivity. They come up with the excuse that it's just the way they are and how they live their lives, therefore it must just be who they are. They usually say, with all due respect, "I'm only a sensitive individual, and I can't change that."

Emotional sensitivity often results in incapacitating states filled with tension, worry, and despair.

It's also crucial to understand that there is no room for forgiveness if your actions or mindset just make you vulnerable, helpless, and incapable of controlling yourself. Not when suffering is the only thing you get in return. In essence, sensitive people have a wider perspective on life. They are significantly better at haggling when using their wants and environment as leverage. On the other hand, delicate people are emotionally restrained.

Additionally, this trait will often be a sign of many more serious fundamental problems. We're talking about things like demanding disorders, anxiety, terrible emotional management, etc. We should spend a little more time delving into this subject because of this.

Emotional Fragility: Root Causes and Symptoms

A few of years ago, the American College Health Association published a fascinating study on emotional sensitivity. They spoke about a very worrying statistic: children nowadays are far more distressed, stressed, and emotionally dependent. To top it all off, this age group also has far greater rates of attempted suicide. Behind this measurement, there is an obvious emotional delicacy hiding. There is a glaring shortage of resources for handling even the most common problems.

A significant part of these mental disorders have childhood trauma as their underlying causes. Few families have been aware in recent decades that our population has started to demand an ever-increasing number of competencies. Because of this, parents now have to work much harder to encourage their kids to think critically, even while they're still very young.

To assure their success, they try to provide them with every resource imaginable. They constantly remind them of how unique they are and how they must develop properly, which motivates them to go above and beyond expectations. All of it is OK. In any event, they're missing a few important nuances with that strategy.

The most important one is that parents protect their children from disappointment. These kids find it challenging to learn how to make decisions on their own. They experience insecurity and find it quite difficult to control their own emotions. They gradually come to realize that they are not really "uncommon" to everyone else. They are aware that they lack the necessary resources, tools, or tactics to handle even the most pressing problems. We're going to look at the typical traits of people who are sensitive to emotions right now.

How would I be able to tell whether I have an emotional sensitivity?

Some of the traits of someone with emotional sensitivity include:

incapacity to understand and process emotions such as sympathy, wrath, irritation, and so forth... They typically overreact to this kind of emotion.

a persistent feeling of emptiness.

feeling overwhelmed by fundamental difficulties, disagreements, or any situation that doesn't turn out the way they expected.

unable to control your annoyance.

having trouble taking charge of their own lives. inclining to think that everything is too much for them.

their ongoing societal problems. they get the impression that everyone around them is lying or betraying them.

Low energy, detached, and constant despondency.

They seem uneasy because they take on just about any task. They lack confidence and feel inadequate.

Every now and again, when things don't turn out the way they expected, people react violently or fiercely.

Your emotional health typically depends on your upbringing and the quality of your first interpersonal relationships. In any event, a toxic upbringing or ineffective education are not the end. There is always time to overcome emotional sensitivity.

Techniques for enhancing emotional stability and self-confidence:

Imagine a porcelain cup if you need to understand the process of becoming emotionally solid. You understand how delicate it is. Even the breaks from prior breaks are still clearly visible. That porcelain cup, however, is most certainly not delicate. It is beautiful despite its form, substance, and several minor imperfections.

Generally speaking, you may allow yourself to be sensitive, but not delicate. Avoid crossing the path where you end up shattering your whole being. Don't allow your inner greatness, principles, or personality escape you. But how would you go about doing that? How would you get rid of the delicate that makes you unhappy?

Get aware of your emotional deficiencies as a first step. We're talking about all the empty spots that lead to problems and are inconvenient. Although it may seem like a strange approach, studies have shown that handicraft therapy may really be quite effective for this. Using colors, canvases, and sketches to explore your thoughts, emotions, and inner concerns is a wonderful technique.

Take personal responsibility for your actions as the next stage. Delicate people often believe that they are the victims of their illness, society, or others around them. All they ever do is react, like a ball bouncing back and forth between two solid walls. You need to take charge and develop a sincere, audacious feeling of responsibility rather than just reacting.

This obligation also entails letting go of the past and making adjustments in the present. All advancements include some level of fear, but if you can remove those obstacles from your daily life, you'll be able to see how much more secure you have become. At long last, you have self-control.

Finally, we must emphasize that this is a complicated process. It often requires the support of a competent therapist to complete the journey. Remember that, despite how difficult it may appear, you always have the option of developing emotional stability. can modify your porcelain cup so that it becomes an exceptional, sturdy, and beautiful work of art.

The 'Shadow Self' of a Highly Sensitive Person Is a Narcissist

People with narcissistic personality disorder, often known as narcissists, have an unconscious belief that they are superior to others. That leads to a need for approval, admiration, and usually wealth or renown as well as a complete lack of empathy for the needs of others. A person who will manipulate or use others to further their goals is an outcome.

However, being a highly sensitive person is perfectly fine and has nothing to do with one's self-image. People who are very sensitive have sensory systems that deeply process all information, from sights and sounds to thoughts and emotions. In general, they will have imagination, mindfulness, and mind. They might also easily get overwhelmed since such preparation leads to overstimulation.

What do these two shares really mean in practice? Nothing, in the grand scheme. Additionally, they are almost perfect opposite energies in one keyway: compassion.

High affectability, however, mostly concerns how you use data. Actually, the majority of HSPs are really understanding. Indeed, the parts of the brain associated with compassion are far more active in HSPs than in non-HSPs, and HSPs will, in general, be nurturing givers who practice philanthropy.

Since the narcissist lacks empathy, he or she is essentially the HSP's "shadow self."

Why would someone who is thoughtful and sensitive need to be friends with someone who has no sympathy at all? They wouldn't, on the surface, but at that point, narcissists don't really go around with signs that read, "I Want to Use You." In actuality, they do the opposite: Many narcissists learn how to seem alluring, kind, and flattering in order to hide their tendencies. (Critically, this is mostly ignorant — like virtually everything that characterizes a narcissist. Typically, they are unaware that they are doing it.) Many may even "love bomb" the people they need to be close to, making them feel good around the narcissist and preventing them from running away like an addict.

Anyone may get caught, HSP or not.

HSPs are unique since their own increased degree of compassion suggests that they are drawn to helping and caring for others. The narcissist also has a constant need to be taken into account, including the need for praise, special favors, regard, and — most crucially — constant consoling. Aside from that, while having exceedingly lofty ambitions, they are often upset, disheartened, or even excessively angry since nothing they do or achieve will ever be sufficient. Is there not anybody who can treat them with the respect they deserve?

In fact, regrettably, and rather often, it's an HSP, the person who keenly feels the suffering of others and derives real satisfaction from making a difference. HSPs are often the first to provide assistance and consolation to someone in need, which puts them at danger of being led into a narcissist's trap.

This may quickly lead to an unequal relationship where the narcissist benefits from all of an HSP's compassion, empathy, love, and often, untold hours of their time. However, the HSP just becomes more and more exhausted. They could run across a barrage of oddities, feel-bad gatherings, annoying attacks, and indignation.

Furthermore, they will learn that there aren't enough empathic people, no matter how much they do.

Integrity and resilience are linked

Because narcissists are expert manipulators, it is difficult to keep a safe distance from their influence. How can narcissistic abuse victims take care of themselves?

There are ways to get free of the suffering. Realizing they are victims is the first step.

Be aware that those who experience mental torture often exhibit certain characteristics. They may move on from their relationships once they recognize these traits.

Various Victims

Witnessing such repressive behavior will aid victims. Knowing if they are the kinds of individuals who are likely to become sources of what analysts refer to as Narcissistic Supply is a reference to a source of self-esteem support for narcissists.

1. Empathetic

Empaths are first on the list. These folks are humble, which is usually a good thing. However, because of their inclination to bring themselves down, they are easy pickings for narcissists.

Empaths are easy targets because they give up on themselves. They see it as their obligation to contribute. They are unaware that narcissists would take from them without asking for anything in return. They must now take precautions to protect themselves.

2. People who are low in self-esteem

Narcissistic abuse is also more likely to occur in those who have poor self-esteem. Because of their restrictive views, narcissists may easily lay the blame at their feet. In general, people will reject it because they believe they deserve the treatment.

3. The Beat Up

These people have previously been narcissists' victims. They tolerate it because they've become used to receiving bad treatment. They are clear targets for abusers because of this.

4. The severely depressed

Neurosis is more likely among anxious people. They are hence suitable for gaslighting. Narcissists may easily convince them that their behavior is unacceptable.

5. People who are easily discouraged

In a similar vein, being discouraged renders one available for plucking. They have become used to the negativity and allowed it to continue, much like the people who are drained.

6. Kids you don't like

Finally, those who were neglected by their parents while they were teenagers are more likely to engage in narcissistic abuse. They may cherish the attention they get from anybody, including narcissists, since they seek for adulation.

7. People who rely on each other

Victims who are in mutually reliant relationships with narcissists will believe it is challenging to seize their chance again. Codependency occurs when the two groups unintentionally feel responsible for one another. While victims endure excruciating verbal and even physical abuse, narcissists may believe that their compatriots don't fulfill their requirements.

Continuing after Narcissistic Abuse

Adapting to situations like NVS is a long-drawn out process, but it's crucial. Without doing so, victims would always feel exhausted and lacking in faith. How may they ultimately continue living their lives?

1. Acknowledge the abuse

Most significantly, pestering must be seen by the victims. To help people recognize its symptoms, they should ask themselves questions.

If their friends or allies are narcissistic abusers, they will usually interrupt or store conversations.

Additionally, they will often disregard boundaries and violate social norms.

Their inflated personalities would sustain; they continuously demanded special treatment.

A tendency to exert control is one of a narcissist's characteristics. They take advantage of their allies for their own gain.

2. Refrain from attempting to influence the abuser.

Additionally, victims should take all necessary precautions to avoid forcing narcissists to change since they are unlikely to feel the need to improve their flaws. They must take all necessary measures to prevent their relationships from becoming better since trying to persuade stubborn narcissists would be fruitless. Love and kindness are ineffective.

3. Attempt to control your anger against the narcissist.

Finally, victims should stop feeling sorry for their narcissistic partners since their empathy would serve as a source of narcissistic inventory. It would help narcissists and make their behavior worse.

Narcissistic abuse victims don't have to go through unending emotional suffering. They should choose the best course of action for themselves once they realize that they are prospective narcissistic stockpiling.

Signs You are a Narcissist's Victim.

Is it accurate to say that you are dating a person who has narcissistic personality disorder? If this is the case, you probably fell victim to narcissistic abuse. Continue reading to look for clues.

1. You're Feeling Down

When your partner constantly criticizes you, it's hard to be upbeat. If all you come across are carelessness and cynicism, chances are you're in a miserable state.

Indicators of sorrow include: feeling unpleasant and ashamed; losing interest; feeling more anxious than usual; having trouble falling asleep or staying asleep; being irritable; and changing weight.

You may have an emotional and mental downturn as a result of suffering. In the event that you start to feel self-destructive, it could be best to seek professional help.

2. Your partner undermines your confidence

Narcissists are notorious for lowering other people's self-esteem.

Your partner might take advantage of you if you don't believe in yourself. It is much easier to dominate you if you believe that your partner is superior to you.

You probably feel as if you can't escape this unpleasant reality if your sense of self-worth has taken a hit.

3. Everything You Do Is Insufficient

No matter what you do, it's seldom enough. Your accomplice gains popularity by corrupting and discrediting you.

If your accomplice supports anything you do, he or she is releasing some pressure. Ask these questions to yourself.

- Is my helper unaware of my accomplishments?

- Does my partner ever express negativity?

- Is my helper opposed to praising my actions?

If you answered "yes" to any of these questions, you have been the victim of narcissistic abuse.

4. You're Persuaded You're losing it.

A narcissist will imply that your thoughts are incorrect by what they say and how they say it. Your partner will try to convince you that it's all in your head as you start to realize how clear the situation is.

Gaslighting is the term for this technique. Your accomplice will purposefully give you the impression that you are losing your mind.

By gaslighting you, your accomplice might gain a lot more power.

5. It's Hard to Get Out

You've allocated time to give it careful thought. You've discussed everything with a close friend. Similar to that, your accomplice draws you back in just as you're about to depart.

Narcissists are experts at pushing their partners as far as they can go. When you decide that enough is enough, your companion turns into a wad of appeal.

When you have to go, you get all the love and respect. In any case, you are ignored if you stay.

Anxiety Disorder Borderline

Borderline individuals can come across as being highly impulsive. The most terrifying aspect of someone with this illness is that they exhibit rapid, dramatic emotional swings without prior notice.

They could adore you one day and detest you the next, and both poles can be quite far apart. For others around them, these individuals are often quite emotional in response to circumstances that don't seem warranted, which may be very perplexing. They often exhibit very depressed mental states, or they may abruptly go from dread to rage. They may have unjustified dread of things happening to them or anger about events taking place nearby that they may see as an assault. They seem emotionally unbalanced and too sensitive to what are mostly fictitious dangers.

The borderline person's lack of awareness that their own conduct is unreasonable and upsetting to others, along with this illogical behavior, makes the problem much worse. They really think that the other person—whoever that may be; most often, it is their spouse—is the issue. They will hold the other person accountable, furious, and despised. They won't be able to or want to admit that their actions in any way contributed to the issue. They are really challenging to deal with since they lack ownership or understanding.

It's interesting to note that women are far more likely than males to have borderline personality disorder. This may be because it is an emotional pattern, and women are more likely than males to experience intense emotional patterns. However, the condition may affect both men and women.

You may be thinking to yourself, "Does my spouse have a borderline personality disorder?" while you read this. You may find out by asking the following questions to yourself:

Do I believe that, in our marriage, I can never be certain of my spouse's state of mind at any one time?

Am I never certain of how they will respond to a certain circumstance?

Does my marriage seem like I am always or mostly walking on emotional eggshells, never knowing whether I (or someone else) would be held accountable for anything that we (or they) allegedly done to irritate them?

Being in a relationship with a person who has borderline personality disorder is challenging because of how unpredictable they are. Their responses to events are often illogical and very unexpected. They often overreact to events and frequently have trouble seeing things from someone else's perspective. Additionally, they won't want to accept their own mistakes or those of others. Any perceived disagreement with them will be met with dread or rage.

Simply said, they'll leave their spouse wondering constantly, "What the heck is going on?"

A borderline individual differs significantly from an anxious or insecure one. Although the nervous or insecure person might get highly emotional, they are not nearly as irrational. The worried or insecure individual may sometimes have an emotional outburst, but they will usually settle down very soon and become approachable once again. They won't be terribly unreasonable, but they could be a little irritated. They won't become completely deaf to logic and facts.

However, it may be very difficult, if not impossible, to reason with a borderline personality or simply to have a sensible dialogue. When they believe someone has insulted them or is somehow assaulting them, they have a tendency to have an exceedingly unfavorable opinion of them.

It's crucial to understand that a person with borderline personality disorder won't always express these unpleasant feelings. Another aspect of the illness that makes it very challenging to live with is that. They are often endearing, caring, clever, and a lot of fun to be around. However, one can never predict when the 'switch' will occur. A spouse is constantly reminded that their partner is a fantastic person while they're feeling upbeat and wonders whether "they" are the ones with the issue. How can I eliminate their negative attitudes? Since they're accusing me of it, it must be my responsibility.

Understanding and treating borderline personality disorder

There are several hypotheses put out as to why borderline personality disorder occurs. According to some experts, it could be connected to child abuse. Others suggest a genetic link.

In actuality, nobody is really aware. The study of this issue is still in its infancy, and diagnosis is still not a precise science. The reason could eventually become more obvious.

What should you do, then, if your partner suffers from BPD? Is there a remedy? Is there anything that can be fixed? If not, what is the best way to deal with a borderline individual, particularly in a marriage or close relationship?

The first thing to keep in mind is that maintaining a relationship that even remotely resembles a healthy or "normal" one will be difficult if your partner has borderline personality disorder. This is due to the borderline pattern's tendency to make relationship improvement fairly challenging since the affected individual will continually feel attacked or judged. When you start working with a therapist, ultimately what occurs is that they start to feel threatened by even the therapist. If you choose not to pursue therapy or counseling, it will be exceedingly difficult to make any progress with a therapist or even simply between the two of you.

However, there are a few things you can take action on.

Verify if your partner really has borderline personality disorder before taking any further action if you have any reason to believe they do. It's critical to differentiate between borderline tendencies and the condition itself.

One way to look at it is to ask: "Can my husband or wife acknowledge that they might have issues in this area and are they willing to take ownership of their actions and work to improve?" A therapist can help you discern between the two.

If "Yes," then they most likely just exhibit borderline tendencies. Of course, they will still be challenging to deal with, but at least the chance for improvement is there.

However, if your spouse can only see you as the issue and not themselves at all, then it is very likely that they do in fact have borderline personality disorder. This is especially true if you can see that the problem is severe enough to really be running your entire relationship.

A person with borderline inclinations and someone who really has borderline personality disorder are quite different. More individuals than those who really have the condition exhibit borderline tendencies. However, if you honestly answer the question and give careful consideration to your circumstances, you will know the proper response. When they learn that their partner could have a borderline personality disorder, many individuals experience some anxiety, which might push them into denial. But you will secretly know the truth, and the only way to really advance is by confronting the reality.

If you want to take action after you've shown that your spouse has borderline personality disorder or even simply borderline characteristics, you'll need to bring it up with them. They are the only ones who have the ability to alter their borderline inclinations, after all.

However, attaching a label to them is not a smart idea. You do not want to tell them, "Look, I've been reading about this and I think you have borderline personality disorder." Keep in mind that they will feel assaulted by you, and this will only make the situation worse.

Saying something like, "I've noticed that you have this particular way of thinking or acting that I'm having a hard time dealing with," would be a far more helpful way to address the situation. How about we discuss this trend with someone? How about we speak to someone about what's going on there and see how we can go on in our marriage? You seem to have this tendency, and I seem to have a habit of finding it hard to deal with.

You can tell whether someone has borderline personality disorder by how negatively they respond to your suggestion. It is, however, the only place to begin. How receptive they are to discussing these concerns must be apparent.

Unfortunately, you only have two choices if your spouse refuses to accept responsibility for their issue (which, as you have undoubtedly recognized by now, they definitely won't do if they have a full-blown case of borderline personality disorder). I wish there were alternative possibilities, but they don't seem to be accessible, so none of them may be really enticing.

The awful irony is that if your spouse suffers from a severe form of borderline personality disorder, they will never take action to address it since they won't admit they have a problem. As a consequence, they are incurable. This condition is one of the most painful and damaging circumstances for any relationship because of this.

Knowing that, you have two choices:

Option 1: Accept it and live with it.

As you learn more about your spouse's health, you may be able to come up with coping mechanisms. Naturally, you will have to accept that they are incurable, that they will continue to act irrationally for which they will never accept responsibility, and that you will bear the lion's share of the burden. Life will always be an emotional and dramatic roller coaster. Finding strategies to maintain your sanity is necessary if you are unable or unable to end your marriage. These could include scheduling frequent separations from your spouse and seeking out outside help (from friends, relatives, or even a counselor or therapist).

But I'll be straight with you: never expect to be completely happy. I'm sorry to be the one to break the bad news to you, but being in a relationship with someone who has BPD implies that your level of communication will never be at a genuinely healthy or profound level. You will find yourself becoming less and less able to be open and honest because of the continual danger of their "swinging" attitude.

Option #2: Divorce your spouse

Perhaps there isn't a better choice than this. The benefit of choice #2 over option #1 is that at least you offer yourself a chance for happiness in the future. If you decide to leave, your borderline spouse won't like it. In fact, you will be held responsible for anything that has 'wrong' in your marriage, and they could respond harshly. I've seen questionable situations in which the individual got hell-bent on killing their spouse, even at the expense of their own health. This is obviously done to convince themselves that they are the ones with problems and that the spouse who wants to leave is to blame for everything. Why would they want to depart? There is nothing wrong with me. Do they not realize how much I cherish them? We could solve our issues if they would just strive harder. They don't seem to care at all about me, therefore there must be something wrong with them. They are very self-centered. These are the borderline personality's mental processes while contemplating the dissolution of their marriage.

Attention Seekers

Few people are more utterly dependent than the narcissist. These folks need constant and undivided attention from everyone.

They resemble young toddlers in many ways. Tantrums, pouting, and unceasing sobbing are all common behaviors. You will get into problems or be soon replaced by someone who does if you somehow fail to provide the required attention.

You will be acquainted with the phrase "love bombing" if you have done any research on the subject of narcissism.

It's crucial to understand that they are not acting in this way because they are madly in love with you.

They don't have feelings for you. They are really working very hard to get all of your attention because they think you would be a good fit to provide them with a service. However, you must get addicted before you will be most eager to start working. This is because, at the end of the day, you will be expected to labor for nothing.

They want your undivided attention and your addiction to their attention. They'll have all you have once you secure this.

similar to when someone purchases a lapdog. They first give the puppy a ton of love and care in the hopes that doing so would help the dog bond with them and develop romantic feelings for them.

The offering of attention becomes something that is only shown when the owner feels like it after this dog is comfortable and giving plenty of unconditional affection.

In other words, the dog is there because of the owner, not the other way around.

Regardless of how much the owner claims to adore the dog. They just leave the dog behind and go to locations that do not permit the dog.

similar to when the dog unintentionally bites them.

Despite the fact that it was an accident on the side of the animal, the wrath is genuine and instantaneous.

However, if the puppy bothers them, they just scoot it aside without giving the dog any thought or consideration.

The same is true of narcissists when it comes to people.

When they need you for anything or if it suits them, they will pay attention to you. You will be left in the cold if they decide that doing so is inconvenient or unnecessary.

But you will always need to show them your love, affection, and devotion. People often claim that narcissistic individuals lack empathy, but there is really a lot more going on. Like a toddler, the narcissistic person is exclusively concerned with their own emotions.

They don't consider how their activities affect you or care about how you feel about them. It doesn't matter whether you're joyful, depressed, or completely devastated. How you make them feel is the sole factor that matters throughout and will always be crucial.

Along with how people feel in general, this. They are not emotionless as a result; rather, they are primarily concerned with their own feelings and not those of others. They'll depend on you to continually fuss, take care of, and strain yourself for them. You're supposed to laugh off humiliation and accept being the punchline when it's convenient for them.

not to express an opinion and not to take any action without, if possible, first getting their consent.

must constantly adore them and be totally focused on them. They have a desire to have control over you personally as well as your whole existence.

They will continue to make an effort to get your attention even after you have lost interest in them or a scenario with them.

For them, negative attention is just as beneficial as positive attention since attention is attention.

As a result, the narcissistic person is fundamentally highly insecure. Something is wrong when a person constantly wants another person or people to swoon over them.

We all like receiving affirmation, but there must be a serious issue when we require it all the time.

What A Narcissist-Involved Relationship Is Like

Are you someone's son, daughter, spouse, wife, etc.? How would you know for sure if the person you are dating is a narcissist? This section focuses more on how it has been carried out in a relationship and the pattern you would be able to relate to, which will dispel your doubt or strengthen your conviction that your relationship is not narcissistic in nature, even though the pattern adopted in a narcissist relationship may look similar to the techniques discussed above. Ten different models will be explored, but why? to widely encompass.

1. Restrictions on talking about yourself. How frequently are you permitted to

voice your opinions, for instance, as a woman in the home? Hardly ever, or was the last time you even recall it happening? The likelihood that you are dating a narcissist is therefore high. A narcissist prefers to speak about themselves than to let others talk about themselves. At a two-way chat, they scowl. And in this kind of relationship, you have to fight for your views to be heard. But even if you have this chance to express yourself right now. Speculate on what will occur. You can get negative feedback, no attention, or a correction.

Do you often hear the words "but," "actually," or "you see, there is more to it than you can see?" if you are a son? You can always tell when someone feels and behaves as if he is smarter than you. You are without a doubt involved in that kind of connection.

2. You Experience Interruptions Frequently. Don't confuse this with some people's weak communication abilities; they merely interrupt, but that doesn't prevent them from subsequently listening to the other person's point of view. However, the person with whom you are in a relationship will interrupt and take the initiative in the discussion. What's more, he will make the talk about himself. You can see that he isn't really interested in you; you can't be mistaken about this, can you?

Consider the last time you were attempting to tell your husband about a fantastic recognition you received at work, and he grabbed it and began telling what he went through at work that day and how he won people over. This is not desirable. You're right.

3. He disobeys the law. Even though they are little, they don't appear to care. Does your family have guidelines regarding what to do if someone picks up their phone before the end of a meal, for instance? Does he or she breach the law and try to get away with it, or what happens? Is there a regulation governing how a TV is used in your home? In a positive way, how does he or she respond? Or did he never live nearby? You see, a narcissist is interested in breaking the law and certain social conventions.

Stealing other people's possessions, especially office supplies, is another facet of violating the law that has to be looked out for in a rule breaker. Never have they honored the scheduled time. And how often does he violate the law when you are traveling to an event? However, despite the fact that we feel regret for any wrongs we've committed and don't want to return to them, a narcissist won't feel regret or repent for what they've done.

4. Avoid upholding Boundaries. Indeed, everyone has sensations and emotions. Additionally, it is crucial for couples to regard one other's sentiments and emotions, but this does not happen. Instead, they will go too far, take advantage of you, and show little consideration for your preferences or worries.

How often does your partner violate promises and never fulfill his obligations? Additionally, you are not treated with any respect, and if you complain about it, you are accused of being the cause of it. Have a plan; you have been informed that I forgot because of you. If you had reminded me, I wouldn't have forgotten.

5. Pretense of Image. Think about if there is a significant difference in how you are treated in public and private. Any variations? They put on an angelic persona outside before launching their demon persona within. Even worse, how does he do it if they do agree to work with you? Most likely, they're doing it to demonstrate their superiority to you, their uniqueness relative to you, and a host of other things.

Six. They Feel Entitled. How does he or she want to be treated by you? You wouldn't ever get a little piece in return if you gave him special treatment. They believe that they are the center of the universe and that you should give them more thought than they will give to you.

7. They Can Persuade People. Do you only experience love during sexual encounters and when someone needs a favor from you? Once the period is through, they will probably return to their original mode, and you finally become accustomed to it. In their minds, you capture their attention just as they need you to and then, just as quickly, you become so repulsive that you are no longer a force to be reckoned with.

You are undoubtedly in a narcissist relationship if your father or your spouse often only interacts with you when they need to satisfy their own wants and demands that you give him your whole attention.

8. A haughty personality. Has he or she ever informed you that you need him to survive? If so, it's likely that he feels the same way. The spouse needs the other to complete their love, yet acting in a way that makes you feel unimportant hurts your self-esteem. The success of a project you are both working on is not shared. Instead, they claim credit for the project's success.

9. Unfavorable feelings. Despite being in a relationship, they could unnecessarily distribute negative information about you to others. They do this too, but there is a limit. However, if you defy their wishes or disagree with their opinions at home, they throw fits. And you don't

even dare contradict him or her because they would shoot back.

Your partner is implicitly degrading you if they judge and make fun of you in front of others on a frequent basis. They make you feel inferior in order to feed their frail ego.

10. In charge of all decision-making. Have you ever been given the freedom to make a split-second decision? They are still debating whether to decide. Additionally, they continue to decide without taking into account who you are or what you stand for in order to appease them. You cannot abandon your point of view and must submit to their rules and regulations.

A narcissist is a really wicked person, and relationships with them are not the greatest. It has the ability to slowly kill and incapacitate a person over time. Now, can you see yourself dating a narcissist? Fine! The information below will assist you in avoiding such scenario without harming either yourself or the narcissist!

A Narcissist's Telltale Behavior

So how can one spot a narcissist? The narcissist's obvious feeling of entitlement is the first thing that stands out. They demand that they be treated with the great respect due to their rarity, specialness, and importance. Narcissists exhibit arrogance because they believe they are flawless. Because it requires work to maintain such self-perception, a narcissist must minimize the merits and accomplishments of others in order to do this. You may be sure narcissism is the driving force behind someone who is continually disparaging what others do or are. A narcissist must use force to bring others down in order to boost their ego because they cannot bear it when others challenge their own "perfection." Of course, deep-seated feelings of jealousy and insecurity lay at the heart of such conduct, but the narcissist may be too unaware of this knowledge to be aware of it.

A narcissist will simultaneously work to maintain their ego via the interaction of two key psychological defensive mechanisms: projection and introjection. If you're wondering if a narcissist feels guilty about constantly making fun of people in order to maintain their ego, the answer is no. According to Sandy Hotchkiss, a fatal sin of the NPD is shamelessness. The narcissist's lack of shame is insisted upon by the psychotherapist, and this is accomplished via the use of projection. The narcissist casts these flaws or inappropriate behaviors onto others rather from taking a close look at themselves and maybe identifying them. So what exactly is projection? It is one of the most basic forms of protection. People project their own shortcomings onto other people in order to cover them up. They continue to regard themselves as excellent, exceptional, attractive, etc. while having a negative opinion of others owing to attributes they also possess themselves, clouding their vision of both themselves and others.

Additionally, political projection may be a deliberate action. This part of Machiavellian intelligence, which suggests using projection and finger-pointing to obtain political dominance, is crucial.

When it comes to narcissism, introjection is the opposite of projection. The integration of another person's traits or whole personality into one's brain or ego is known as introjection. Introjection that is inspired by feelings of love and maybe loss can also be offensive-free. To make up for it, you may introduce traits, habits, and beliefs from a person you lost. Some folks are able to introduce their spouse or a departed loved one. They only internalize the beliefs and characteristics of the other to make up for the loss or out of a sense of connection. A narcissist, on the other hand, employs introjection in a very specific way: they highlight traits of individuals who could be more successful and respected than they are. You should be aware that you are dealing with a narcissist when you hear someone claim to have qualities that are obviously absent from them but are readily apparent in someone else. They are so elevating and enhancing their own ego at the cost of another person. The narcissist wants to draw attention to themselves and come off as more significant and impressive than they really are, therefore they pretend to have the traits of other people. Of course, they may do this unintentionally as a sort of self-promotion. Their ego just cannot stand the thought of another person holding a position that would win them respect, favor, or notoriety.

A great propensity for exploitation is another essential narcissist trait. The narcissist believes they are entitled to pretty much everything, hence it goes hand in hand with an entitlement mindset. Additionally, they sometimes have success in obtaining their goals by taking advantage of others. People in subordinate roles or those who are innocent, naive, excessively idealistic, and sensitive are most susceptible to being used by narcissists. The narcissist has certain sorts of targets that they perceive as "prey," just as certain types of individuals are destined to be their biggest enemies. You run the danger of being the ideal victim for a narcissist if you don't read people readily or if you don't think most people are mostly decent. Of course, the narcissist is likely to be drawn to characteristics and actions that suggest gullibility, fragility, or a propensity for idealization. They can "smell" potential victims right away. However, since it's a big part of their upbringing, some narcissists may attempt to take advantage of even those who don't show these traits. They feed their egos by demonstrating to themselves that they can control and manipulate just about anybody. Keep in mind that the narcissist feels pressure to live up to an ideal self that is quite different from the self that other people experience. The narcissist's ideal self emphasizes strength, significance, control, trickery, etc. When narcissists can count how many new individuals they have been able to trick and take advantage of, they feel pleased of themselves. A life filled with people they were able to deceive and take advantage of brings comfort to them.

A narcissist may be easily identified by paying careful attention to their relationships and social interactions. Narcissistic support/supply and threats are the two basic types of individuals for the narcissist. While the latter instantly become adversaries since they don't react to the narcissist as intended, the former (willingly or unwillingly) boost their ego. Since the narcissist would flatter and reward their fans in order to keep them active, the narcissistic support may be handled gently (sometimes just in the beginning). Anyone who dislikes or is uninterested in the narcissist is their adversary. As a result, you will be able to recognize significant examples of splitting (black-and-white thinking) in the narcissist's relationships and social interactions. Whatever their true viewpoint, people will naturally be either for them or against them. Those who are eager (or naive enough) to participate in the narcissist's game are considered "friends." All those who contest or refuse to acknowledge the narcissist's power are considered enemies.

You can spot narcissists by their frequent exaggeration of their accomplishments and bragging about how important they think they are because of this. In addition to maintaining their self-image, they do it to win their fans. They will imply that they are significantly superior to most others, very knowledgeable, always correct, and never accountable for anything that goes wrong. They often have opinions that are at odds with reality, therefore looking at the facts can help you spot a narcissist immediately. Even if you're just starting to know someone, you may tell if they're a narcissist if they brag about their achievements yet their accomplishments in life are lacking when you look at the facts. While only depressed and pessimistic individuals concentrate on failure and shortcomings, it's also not typical to entirely overlook such things. A healthy individual is able to recognize and acknowledge both successes and failures. They have a realistic and balanced self-image; they believe they have both fascinating traits and defects, but they don't focus on either. A narcissist may be readily recognized by their whole concentration on positive attributes that are often not genuine.

A history and present count of unsatisfactory or abusive relationships may also help you spot a narcissist. The narcissist will establish untrue connections with those who fit into the "support" category based on flattery and positive reinforcement. Alternately, if the victim is weaker than the narcissist, they may be mistreated and used. Genuine relationships based on affinities and loyalty do not exist with narcissists. Instead, their interactions are often uneven, egotistical, and superficial. Warm or intense interpersonal interactions in which individuals actually care about each other and come to like one other over time are neither possible or appealing to narcissists. Relationships are often instruments that narcissists might use to boost their perception of themselves and their persona in the eyes of others. As you can imagine, a narcissist would boast about others as 'trophies' they were able to get in order to highlight how exceptional and great they are. The narcissist's overt propensity to objectify others makes them easy to spot.

Narcissists have a lot of grandiose illusions, which are often justified by claims of superiority and originality. You can know you're dealing with a narcissist when they are continually bragging about how much admiration they have or how strong, gorgeous, successful, etc. they are. The key is recognizing an excessive emphasis on oneself as opposed to other aspects of one's life, such as their career, family, relationship, etc. The narcissist anticipates that others will share their passion for these illusions. They will get upset or retaliate if they are ignored or criticized. Narcissists want special attention and conformity from everyone, and they are unable to handle criticism, regardless of how constructive it may be. They seem to be acting out a screenplay that is prewritten in their minds and needs a certain sort of criticism. Because of this, when someone acts in accordance with their own personality rather than stroking the narcissist's ego, they will be despised or rejected. The narcissist is unable to comprehend that other people have their own needs for love, admiration, care, and other things; instead, they want unrestricted reverence and favors. You could not exist at all, or you might exist as an extension of the narcissist's ego.

Narcissism might be attractive or ugly on the outside; it doesn't really matter. Their personality condition is caused by a deeper psychological need rather than specific characteristics. That implies that the only way to identify them is by their pompous, arrogant body language. The narcissist is able to reach out to their "public" and possible allies because to their open and attentive nonverbal communication. Aggression and animosity, however, are quite noticeable. The narcissist will occupy space while ignoring all other factors in favor of their quest for "expansion." Regardless of how powerful or threatening they truly seem, their body language will reflect their inflated sense of self. Their nonverbal communication will show arrogance and a desire to dominate. You may immediately begin investigating further behaviors that could be suggestive of NPD if someone shakes your hand in the alleged palm-down fashion, which is meant to imply social dominance. Such conduct is often not an isolated occurrence and may be seen in conjunction with a number of other narcissistic traits. Therefore, aggressive and haughty body language might be a warning indication of narcissism even if you've just met someone or are passing them casually on the street or in a bus.

Remember that NPD isn't always indicated by a person's impactful, assertive, and naturally self-assured body language. True confidence and arrogance vary greatly from one another. The latter requires work to maintain and only superficially resembles the former. The narcissist will approach you using crude inconsistencies. For instance, rather than expressing pure confidence or beauty, their body language would scream attention-seeking activity. Even if there isn't much of a reason why they should, narcissists crave attention and to come off as domineering. You may immediately tell you're dealing with a narcissist if someone's body language shouts arrogance and forced superiority and their eyes show hatred, emptiness, or repressed insecurity.

In many ways, narcissists often behave in a unilateral manner. You know you're dealing with a narcissist if, for example, they never pay attention to what you say yet want you to listen intently when they tell a tale about themselves. Additionally, it's a warning sign if you see someone attempting to "steal" the story and spin it about themselves. The technique of continuously turning the (social) emphasis inward is one that narcissists are experts at. In order to get the upper hand over you, the narcissist will immediately bring up something comparable about themselves anytime you express anything great and admirable about you. Of course, it doesn't have to be accurate. Narcissists are unable to interact with others in a way that benefits both parties. If you allow yourself to be sucked into their games and illusions, you are automatically going to lose while you are with them.

The narcissist often places the blame for negative events on someone else. They cannot feel remorse or shame, thus it will only be natural for them to blame the other people. Additionally, narcissists often attribute any negative emotions they experience, such as rage or irritation, to others. Narcissistic wrath is often characterized by lash outs, blaming others, and expecting their demands to be granted. Narcissists feel elated when they come into contact with someone whose mind is more flimsy and porous. They were able to release negative feelings and transfer them to another, which is why this sensation is present. You can plainly see how narcissists often use those who are weaker than them (or at least look to be weaker than them) to bully them in order to vent their irritation and complexes.

Let's look at the many kinds of narcissists you could face now that you understand how to spot them. People wouldn't get caught in codependent relationships with narcissists if they came in a single size and form and if the indications of NPD were so obvious from the beginning. As you'll learn in a later chapter, it's often even too upsetting for the "victim" to realize that they were really only serving the narcissist's ego.

Section 4. A narcissistic abuse is what?

The victim is exposed to narcissistic abuse harm in a kind of viciousness known as narcissistic maltreatment savagery. One of the challenges with narcissistic abuse is that, unlike true cruelty, there are usually not going to be visible scars to serve as evidence. Every moment the victim experiences enthusiastic agony, egotistical cruelty occurs. Narcissistic mistreatment viciousness often includes verbal or physical abuse.

Numerous people suffer from narcissistic abuse and cruelty over time, but they are never aware of it. You would never be able to recognize when you are facing an assault without a true understanding of who you are and what is happening in your life. It also becomes harder to come up with effective ways to deal with the damage caused by such misuse.

While anybody is susceptible to this kind of mistreatment, women and children are the groups most affected by narcissistic abuse. The attacks go after judgments, feelings, and concerns. Although egotistical abuse is unlikely to result in physical harm, the effect on the victim's reputation may be just as damaging.

The casualty may experience a few side effects, reactions, and circumstances in a relationship with a self-absorbed partner that point to abuse. The egotist conditions the victim by setting up interactions with people who have a bad effect on them. Here are some indications that your partner may be mistreating you in a narcissistic way:

Intense instabilities: Your victimizer recognizes your weaknesses and eventually uses them against you. You become even more insecure and are unable to confide in anybody.

Disbelief in oneself – Many victims' lives turn for the worst because they no longer believe in themselves. You are no longer able to trust your judgment since your assurance has been destroyed.

Incapacity - Victims of abuse who were formerly confident and knowledgeable about everything they really do suddenly develop incapacity and uncertainty about everything.

Anxiety causes you to live in constant fear and vulnerability. You always worry that something bad may happen. You have little to no confidence in good things since you understand that happiness is temporary and will soon result in catastrophic events.

Additionally, you have a profound sense of exhaustion and lack of readiness for drawing energy from obvious enjoyment.

Uncertainty - After being grounded, victims become uncertain, confused, and unfit to trust anybody, not even themselves. Esteem problems: Narcissistic abuse and mistreatment erode your self-confidence. You cannot think of yourself as something superior to what your abuser perceives you to be. You stay away from the broader public because you worry that everyone will see your flaws.

www.ingramcontent.com/pod-product-compliance
Lightning Source LLC
Chambersburg PA
CBHW050233120526
44590CB00016B/2069